Contents

Introduction

The history of a town or city may be told in various ways. As well as books and online information, visitors may be able to visit a local history museum or local archives. There may be a marked history trail or other informative displays. Historic buildings may be regularly open to the public and even some of those not normally opened may be visited on 'Open House' weekends.

But there is other history that is not so openly told. There may be industries that have closed down or relocated elsewhere but traces remain, perhaps a building that has received a listed status, a gateway, some industrial machinery that has been preserved as a reminder. There are buildings that may have been repurposed during their lives, with just small clues to their original function – maybe an inscription mounted above eyeline level. There are statues and monuments to commemorate people and events notable at their time but are all but forgotten now.

Then what about place names? In the southern part of the London Borough of Newham we have areas called Silvertown and Canning Town. Was silver ever mined at Silvertown and was there a food canning industry at Canning Town? In the northern part of the borough there are Forest Gate and Manor Park; names that sound as if they have been made up by enterprising estate agents to give a (false) sense of a rural idyll.

Street names too may tell a history, perhaps commemorating some long past personage with links to the area or remembering an industry that used to thrive there.

The London Borough of Newham was created in the 1965 reform of London local government by the merger of the County Borough Councils of East Ham and West Ham, which occupied the closest part of Essex to the City of London itself.

This part of Essex, east of London, grew rich in the nineteenth century from industry, railway engineering and the docks. The continued importance of the area to London's economy was realised by the Luftwaffe who subjected it to heavy bombing in the Second World War.

Much of this industry fell into decline from the late twentieth century and the population was also falling. When the docks closed and relocated to Tilbury, due to new technology like containerisation, the London Docklands Development Corporation was set up to regenerate the Docklands area with London City Airport and a new University of East London campus taking their place. But their remit did not cover the decline of the Stratford area as the railway yards and workshops closed.

However, the borough, once one of London's poorest and most ethnically diverse, has seen a major regeneration, especially since the award of the 2012 Olympic and Paralympic Games to London with the main stadium events held at Stratford. Westfield Shopping Centre was built to accompany this. Now the borough is booming with new housing and other developments, especially around the former Olympic site. More than 9,000 new homes have been created here. The London Legacy Development Organisation was set up to oversee the longer term regeneration of the Olympic Park area and ensure that the Olympics site would not become a 'white elephant'. Part of the site became the Queen Elizabeth Olympic Park, the biggest new London park in over a hundred years. West Ham United FC have moved into the Olympic Stadium, now renamed the London Stadium. Development is ongoing: a new university campus, UCL East, is being built; and a new creative centre opened at East Bank in 2022/23, a joint venture with University College London, London College of Fashion, the BBC, Sadlers Wells and the V&A. The area has even been given its own new postal district – E20. The belated opening of the Elizabeth Line, aka Crossrail, in 2022 has further boosted the area, which, as the council strapline goes, is a place where 'people choose to live, work and stay'.

In this book I want to resurrect some of the forgotten stories that are associated with the industries, buildings, and other artefacts, as well as people, place and street names in an area of East London where I have lived for over sixty years.

1. What's in a Name? Place Names and Street Names

The London Borough of Newham was created in the 1965 reform of London local government by the merger of two of the only three County Borough Councils in the Greater London area – East Ham and West Ham. This meant that they had the same set of powers as a County Council, unlike Borough Councils or Urban District Councils, which had lesser powers than the county they were in and thus certain functions such as education were provided in them by the County Council. When the former boroughs were merged it was decided to call the new London borough Newham, probably so as not to be seen as giving preference to either.

East Ham, West Ham: *Ham* or *hamme* is an Anglo-Saxon word meaning 'a village' or 'dwelling place'. Also *hamm* in Old English meant 'a water meadow'. First recorded in 958 as one place, Hamme, by the end of the twelfth century separate east and west settlements were noted.

DID YOU KNOW?
Until 1965, East Ham and West Ham had their own fire brigades and ambulance services – part of their powers as County Borough Councils.

Beckton: This was named after Simon Adams Beck, governor of the Gas Light & Coke Company, founded in 1870, who built the Beckton Gas Works, the largest in Europe.

Canning Town: Probably named after George Canning who was briefly prime minister in 1827, or his son Charles Canning, first viceroy of India from 1858 to 1862. The area was previously known as Hallsville.

Custom House: The area was named after the Custom House that stood on the north side of the Victoria Docks.

Forest Gate: Derived from a tollgate that kept cattle straying from Wanstead Flats onto local roads. A railway station with this name has existed since first opened by the Eastern Counties Railway in 1840. The tollgate keeper was listed in the 1851 census, but the gate was removed in 1883.

Maryland: Many places in America derive their names from places in Britain – New York, Richmond, Boston, etc. – but here is an unusual example of a place name in London taken from America. In the seventeenth century a merchant named Richard Lee bought land locally after returning from Maryland, Virginia, where he owned a plantation using slave labour. The name is carried by the local railway station on the Elizabeth Line from London to Shenfield. In November 2020 the Newham mayor, Rokhsana Fiaz, called the name 'a disservice to the diversity of the borough' and proposed renaming the area and council ward 'Newtown', but local residents opposed this saying it would undermine their sense of identity.

North Woolwich: *Wic* was an Old English word referring to a village near water. The 'Wool' part of the name may indicate former trading in this product. The 'North' was to distinguish it from the main town of Woolwich on the south side of the river.

> DID YOU KNOW?
> Until 1965, North Woolwich was not administered by East Ham as might be expected but was part of the Borough of Woolwich, based on the south side of the river. Council vehicles would need to cross by the ferry as there were no bridges east of Tower Bridge.

Plaistow: This was recorded as 'Plagestoue' in *c.* 1200. It derives from the Old English *pleg*, meaning 'playing' and *stowe*, 'a place', and so means 'the playing place'.

Silvertown: This name has nothing to do with mining. Around 1850, S. W. Silver opened a factory to make rubber products and built some houses for his workers. Prior to the nineteenth century the area around what is now Silvertown and North Woolwich was an uninhabited marshland called Plaistow Level.

Stratford: From the Old English *straet*, meaning 'road' and 'ford'. Thus, the road with a ford. First recorded in 1177, the ford was over a branch of the River Lea.

Upton Park: Derived from 'up' and Old English *tun* ('a farm'), it means a farm or homestead on higher ground in parkland.

The population of East and West Ham rose rapidly with the growth of industry. From 18,817 in West Ham at the 1851 census to 267,903 in 1901, and 2,858 in East Ham in 1861 to 96,018 in 1901. The population peaked in the 1920s but then fell in the 1950s. But the present century has seen new growth in Newham, from 244,000 in the 2001 census to 308,000 in 2011, a rise of 23.5 per cent, the second highest rise in the country. The 2021 census figure was nearly 384,000. The 2001 census identified Newham as the most ethnically diverse district in England and Wales. It is a predominantly working-class area, including some of the most deprived wards of any London borough. Indeed, in 2004 Newham was ranked the sixth most deprived borough in the whole country, although this will have changed since.

The Borough coat of arms is that of the former West Ham, which features a ship for the docks and crossed hammers for industry, either side of a crozier representing Stratford Langthorne Abbey (founded in 1135). The motto is that from East Ham (but now in English rather than Latin) – 'Progress with the People'.

The former West Ham coat of arms with their motto 'Deo Confidimus' seen on Custom House Library.

DID YOU KNOW?
By the late nineteenth century West Ham was the eighth largest town in Britain. Its population would peak at 300,860 in the 1921 census but declined thereafter until the present century.

Street Names

Some street names commemorate people with local connections. Others may be named after events at the time of their construction. Many of the residential streets date from the turn of the nineteenth to twentieth centuries, hence there are streets in Newham (and elsewhere in London) named after places associated with the Boer War (1899–1902) – e.g. Ladysmith and Mafeking Avenues in East Ham, Ladysmith and Mafeking Roads in West Ham.

One name that used to intrigue me as to its origins was Balaam Street in Plaistow. It is an old name dating back as early as 1371 and taken from a local family, either Balame or Balun.

Some other street names will be explained in later sections of this book.

In recent years Newham Council has added descriptive details to some of their commemorative street names – a commendable service, but perhaps one that makes them less eligible for a book called *Secret Newham*!

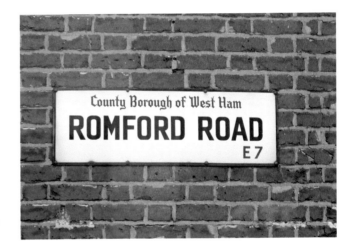

Some old street name signs can still be found with the former County Borough lettering on, such as this one on Romford Road.

Layard Street is a new street in the Stratford City development. It is one of the streets to have been given descriptive details as to the reason for its naming. It also shows the 'E20' postcode created for the former Olympic site area.

2. Industry and Commerce

Before the nineteenth century, most industry would have been concentrated on the banks of the River Lea (or Lee). From early times, as the River Lea neared the Thames it divided into several tidal channels that flowed through marshy areas. The Romans built a ford, Queen Maud built Bow Bridge and in the fourteenth century the abbot of Stratford Langthorne Abbey tried unsuccessfully to divert the river to avoid flooding. In the 1770s various parts of the River Lea between Hertford and London were supplemented by stretches of canal to ease navigation. These included the River Lee Navigation and the Limehouse Cut. The River Lea (Flood Relief) Act 1930 led to extra channels and locks being created, the whole complex being known as the 'Bow Back Rivers'.

Industries included milling, and two tide mills survive in Newham at Three Mills. The House Mill was used by J&W Nicholson & Co. to grind grain for gin production from 1872 until 1940. From *c.* 1744 to 1775 porcelain was made at Bow Pottery on the east side of Bow Bridge.

It was the coming of the railways (see chapter 3), coupled with the rise of new technologies in the Victorian era and legislation prohibiting many of the smellier and noisier industries from operating within London that led to the rapid growth of industry within Newham from the 1840s onwards. In this section I want to feature some of the companies, past and present, that made this part of London their home.

Still in Business

Tate & Lyle

One of the oldest continually functioning businesses in Newham is the Tate & Lyle sugar refinery. There are actually two separate refineries, but why? The clue is in the name. In 1878 Henry Tate opened the Thames Refinery where he pioneered the making of sugar cubes. By 1894 over 2,000 people were employed there. Cane sugar is brought in by ship from Africa, the Caribbean and Pacific countries. Production continued even through the Blitz in the Second World War despite several direct hits. By the end of 2009 the company switched its entire UK retail cane sugars range to Fairtrade. Around 1,000 people, about half of whom are contractors, are employed there. The ships that bring the raw sugar at the rate of around thirty ships a year are now the only large cargo ships to travel this far upriver since the closure of the docks in the 1970s and 1980s. Originally the cane sugar was transported in bags but is now shipped in bulk. The company invested in new grab cranes for unloading in 2007 at a cost of some £3 million, thus showing their commitment to the river. It remains the largest sugar refinery in Europe.

On 13 March 2008 the Elizabeth II and the Duke of Edinburgh visited the refinery to celebrate 130 years of production, and she unveiled a plaque in the main yard. She saw the company's educational resource centre, which has displays of how sugar was originally sold.

A little further upriver in West Silvertown is a second refinery, Plaistow Wharf, which opened in 1881 and is also owned by Tate & Lyle. This was the plant of Abram Lyle. In 1885 he created Lyle's Golden Syrup, a sugar by-product, and still sold today in the same distinctive tins with the lion motive and the slogan 'Out of the strong came forth sweetness'. The two manufactures merged in 1921. Both made fortunes from their products and like so many of their contemporaries they were great philanthropists, giving back to the community, although it is believed that they never actually met. Tate amassed an art collection, which he bequeathed to the nation as the National Gallery of British Art, which opened in 1897. In 1932 it became the Tate Gallery and is now the Tate Britain. Abram Lyle created Lyle Park by the river in Silvertown. It was this refinery that received substantial damage in the Silvertown explosion (see p. 62).

Both refineries remain in use in 2022, although production levels have declined in recent years. Tate & Lyle has been owned by ASR Sugars of America since 2010.

Polish Steamship Co. *Podlasie* discharges at Thames Refinery on 20 January 2022.

Tate & Lyle's other refinery at West Silvertown – home of Lyle's Golden Syrup.

Thomas Cribb & Sons

Established in 1881, Thomas Cribb & Sons is an independent family firm of funeral directors, now run by the fourth and fifth generation of the family. They offer a range of services including motorised and horse-drawn funerals and serve an area throughout east London and south Essex. Their headquarters are at Beckton.

At the entrance to their Beckton headquarters there is road named after the founder of the company – Thomas Cribb Mews.

This mural photo formerly on the wall of their headquarters shows the original premises.

The unique Who Shop at Nos 39–41 Barking Road, Upton Park, E6.

The Who Shop

One of the most unique businesses in Newham, the Who Shop is a specialist retailer dealing in all things relating to *Doctor Who*. It was started by wife and husband team Alexandra and Kevan on 1 December 1984 at a warehouse in Wapping. It then moved to a location on Station Parade, High Street North, opposite East Ham station, until moving to the present site in 2009. The shop sells a wide range of merchandise including magazines, themed clothing, gifts and original scripts and props. The staff also attend various conventions and events worldwide. In addition, there is a museum (entry via a TARDIS, of course!) featuring over 120 different props, costumes and artefacts from the *Doctor Who* series and its spin-offs since 1964. A photo wall documents the stars from the show who have visited. There is an admission charge for the museum and details of opening hours are on the website: www.thewhoshop.com.

No Longer in Business:

Beckton Gas Works

Beckton Gas Works was the biggest in the world. Started in 1868 and opened by the Gas Light & Coke Company in 1870, when fully developed it covered an area larger than the 'square mile' of the City of London. It was named after the first governor, Simon Adams Beck (1803–83). The coal was delivered by ship and unloaded by hydraulic cranes to be conveyed to the retort houses. As well as coal gas, coke, dyes and fertilizers were produced as by-products. The works had an extensive internal railway network serving both the retort houses and the by-products plants. It was worked by a number of 0-4-0 tank locos in green livery for the main works, red for the by-products plant. These were of cut-down design because of low clearances. The GL&CC amalgamated with some of its less efficient rivals such as the Imperial Company who had works at Bromley-by-Bow. By 1945 it accounted for 12 per cent of total national gas sales. Following nationalisation of the gas industry in 1948–49, Beckton came under the ownership of the North Thames Gas Board.

DID YOU KNOW?
The disused remains of Beckton Gas Works were used to represent bombed-out Vietnam in certain scenes of the 1987 film *Full Metal Jacket* directed and produced by Stanley Kubrick.

Beckton closed in 1969 following the discovery of North Sea Gas. The site was very polluted so at first was left untouched. Then the waste tip known locally as the 'Beckton Alps' was landscaped and covered in a layer of clay and a ski slope was opened there in 1989 by Princess Diana. A Norwegian firm submitted plans to build 'Snow World', an indoor real snow ski slope, at a cost of between £20 million and £35 million. They started to build the foundations but punctured the layer of clay that covered the toxic core. As a result, the site was declared unsafe, the plans fell through and the site was closed and fenced off in 2001. At the corner of Winsor Terrace and Tollgate Road an Asda superstore and bus station opened in 1983. This area was subsequently developed with housing and local facilities. The second phase of the Docklands Light Railway saw it extended to Beckton in March 1994, which has encouraged further development. Since then, the rest of the gasworks site has been cleared. Gallions Reach Shopping Park, a maintenance depot for the Docklands Light Railway, various logistics sites and housing development have taken its place, although there are still patches of undeveloped land interspersed among these.

So, what remains of the former Beckton Gas Works? There is the 'Beckton Alps' site of course. Winsor Terrace was once a private road owned by the gasworks. At the end of Winsor Terrace is a set of gates that led into the gasworks. There is also a terrace of houses that were built to house workers of the company. These contrast with the new housing built since closure. The Winsor name is also commemorated by a local primary school. One gasholder remains in situ to remind us of the former industry. Also, within the entrance lobby to the original Asda shopping centre is a mural picture of the gasworks blacksmith's shop. On the Thames, the supports of the pier where coal was unloaded can still be seen.

Winsor Terrace, named after Friedrich Winzer who founded the Gas, Light & Coke Company in 1812. It was originally a private road owned by the company who built houses there for their employees. Some of these houses were destroyed during the Second World War but others still remain, along with more modern counterparts.

At the end of Winsor Terrace; these gates once led to the Beckton Gas Works.

These pillars still remain in place from the former pier on the Thames where colliers once unloaded the coal for gas production.

The ski slope at Beckton Alps during a spell of real snow, 14 February 1991. (Photo courtesy of Newham Archives, Newham Heritage Service)

This large photo mural is installed in the entrance to the Beckton Asda shopping centre, depicting a blacksmith's shop at the former gas works.

18

Bromley-by-Bow Gasworks

This gasworks was built by the Imperial Gas Light & Coke Company to compete with the
GL&CC Beckton works. Coal was delivered to a new canal dock, later named Cody Dock.
It opened in 1873 but was not a financial success as most of the surrounding area was
already supplied by the GL&CC and as a result was sold to them in 1876. The gasworks
lasted until 1976, although latterly only used for storage.

The former GL&CC offices in
Twelvetrees Crescent, built in 1905.
This later housed the London Gas
Museum until it closed *c.* 1998.

Outside the offices is this
monogram of the GL&CC.

By the GLCC offices is Memorial Park. Originally a private park of the company, it is now open to the public. There is a war memorial to company employees and a statue to Sir Corbet Woodall (1841–1916), engineer of the gasholders and later chairman of the GL&CC. This was moved here from Beckton after its closure. There is also a perpetual flame, originally gas and now electric.

Seven of the original eight Grade II listed gasholders survive and some were in use from 1873 until closure. In 2023 a planning application was made for a new housing development on this site with the restoration of the gasholders.

Dane

The Dane Group of Companies on Stratford High Street/Sugar House Lane started in 1853 and closed in 2005. They made paint, ink and pigments and were the largest producer of Day-Glo pigments in the world.

Yardley

This building in Stratford High Street is the only surviving part of the former Yardley soap and perfumes business. The company had built a factory in Carpenters Road in 1904. Additional land in Stratford High Street was acquired in 1918 for storage, distribution and box making. This art deco building was designed by Higgins & Thomerson in 1937. In 1963 Yardley were refused permission to expand the site at Stratford and instead took out a lease on a site at Basildon, Essex, to which they moved in 1966.

Some other industries that have now disappeared include Berk Spencer Acids near West Ham station, and John Knight's Royal Primrose Soap Works, opened at Silvertown in 1880. Many older people will probably remember Knights Castille soap. Also at Silvertown was the rubber firm S. W. Silver & Co., founded in 1852, which gave the area its name, and the chemical company Brunner Mond, whose factory would be destroyed in the Silvertown explosion of 1917 (see p. 62). There were also factories making inter alia creosote, glue and plywood. You may note a common theme of dirty, noisy, smelly and polluting industries and there is a reason for this. In 1844 the Metropolitan Building Act restricted many such industries from operating in the counties of London and Middlesex. Hence these industries located eastward into the nearest part of Essex over the border which was at Bow Creek. By 1910 only Bristol had more factories south of Birmingham.

The Dane Group made ink here
[1853 - 2005] and this was the owner's dog.

DANE'S YARD

established in 1853

Above: All that
remains of the
former Dane site
is this sign, now
with an explanatory
notice.

Right: The art deco
former Yardley
building in Stratford
High Street.

In 1913 Yardley purchased an engraving of Francis Wheatley's *The Flower Sellers*, which became their trademark, and it is this tiled image that is the distinguishing feature of the building.

Stratford Co-operative and Industrial Society Ltd

The Stratford Co-operative and Industrial Society Ltd was started by a group of men at Stratford Railway Works in 1862. The Co-operative movement had begun in Rochdale in 1844. The first premises of the Stratford Co-op were on the corner of Falmouth Street and Maryland Street in Stratford. In 1929 the Stratford Co-op amalgamated with the Edmonton Co-op to form the London Co-operative Society.

H.M. James & Sons Ltd, Manor Park

H. M. James & Sons at No. 736 Romford Road, Manor Park, specialised in bathrooms and bathroom fittings, in particular discontinued models and colours. Founded in 1880, they lasted 137 years until closed on 29 September 2013. After their closure much of the stock and the domain name were acquired by the Bathing Machine (Pontefract) Limited.

This plaque survives on a building on High Street South/Mitcham Road, East Ham. Opened in 1913, it used to be a Co-op grocery but now belongs to another grocery chain.

The former premises of H. M. James & Sons after closure and before new signage was erected by the replacing occupants.

Sometimes evidence of a past industry or business is briefly uncovered during redevelopment. In November 2020 the former premises of the long-standing Romford Electrical Services Ltd (founded 1958) in Manor Park were being redeveloped when the shopfront sign was removed to reveal this former signwriting beneath. An hour or so after I photographed this it had been boarded over.

Elsewhere a more permanent reminder may be a painted wall sign from a former business, such as this on the end of a row of houses in Boxley Street, Silvertown, E16, fronting onto a garage. J&J Downey Ltd were an engineering company. Note the phone number ALB 4276-7 (i.e. Albert Dock), which dates from before 1966–70, after which numbers replaced letters to represent the phone exchanges. This 'ghost sign' is readily visible from the Docklands Light Railway.

3. Railways and Road Transport

Stratford Station, Works and Loco Depot

East London was the commercial and industrial side of the capital. So, it was not surprising that when railways were developed, east London was at the forefront. In fact, the first passenger railway in London was the London & Greenwich line, running along the south side of the Thames from London Bridge to Greenwich, reached in 1838. The north bank soon followed, with the first section of the Eastern Counties Railway opening in 1839. This later merged with other railways to become the Great Eastern Railway in 1862, the main railway company serving East Anglia. Services terminated in London at Shoreditch from 1840 (renamed Bishopgate in 1846). The present terminus at Liverpool Street did not open until 1874. Stratford first became a junction as early as 1840 when the Northern & Eastern Railway line from Broxbourne joined here.

A line to North Woolwich opened in 1847 and another to Loughton in 1856, later extended to Epping and Ongar. The low-level platforms opened in 1854 as part of a link extending the North Woolwich line northwards to connect with the North London Railway at Victoria Park.

The GER was merged into the London & North Eastern Railway (LNER) in 1923, and this in turn would be incorporated into the nationalised British Railways in 1948.

The Great Eastern Railway, faced with threats from competing trams, had considered electrification in the early twentieth century but were unable to afford the cost. A new proposal to electrify the suburban services from Liverpool Street to Shenfield came in 1935 under the New Works Programme, a government series of public investment projects partly to relieve unemployment in the Depression. Major engineering works included the rebuilding of Stratford station and a flyover at Ilford to separate suburban and main line tracks. A new depot was constructed at Ilford to maintain the electric trains.

Electric services to Shenfield started from 26 September 1949 with a full service in 1950. Fenchurch Street station was electrified along with the connecting link from Bow Junction with the intention of running a shuttle service between Fenchurch Street and Stratford, but this was dropped as an unnecessary duplication of the new Central line and the new bay platforms 4 and 7 at Stratford were not commissioned.

Also under the New Works Programme, the route from Stratford to Epping and Ongar and the Hainault loop were transferred to London Transport to become an extension to the Central line. Work started in the 1930s but was suspended during the war, continuing thereafter to Stratford (1946) and Epping (1949).

Electrification has since been extended in stages to cover all the main line to Norwich and most of the branches under British Railway's Modernisation Plan and also following the implications of the Clean Air Act. East Anglia would become the first part of BR to eliminate steam in 1962.

DID YOU KNOW?
In November 2021 Stratford was reported as Britain's busiest railway station.

In February 1978 the BR chairman, Sir Peter Parker, announced improvements to the North London Line, including investment in the North Woolwich line, and the reopening to passengers of the Stratford–Dalston line with new stations to create a through North Woolwich to Richmond route. Passenger services on this line had been withdrawn in 1944. The Greater London Council would fund this electrification on the basis of the social benefits it would bring to an area needing redevelopment. New stations were built at Dalston Kingsland in 1983 (replacing Dalston Junction), Hackney Central (1980), Hackney Wick (1980) and Homerton (1985). Through electric services commenced between North Woolwich and Richmond from 13 May 1985, marketed as 'North London Link'.

The next addition to Stratford's railway network was the Docklands Light Railway, the first section of which opened in 1987 (see p. 32).

A new Stratford station building opened on 14 May 1999, a fitting building for this location's increasingly important role as an interchange. In the same year the station gained another new Underground line: the Jubilee Line Extension from Green Park via Docklands, which opened just in time to serve the Millennium Exhibition at the new Millennium Dome at North Greenwich (since renamed the O2 Arena).

Stratford had been home to locomotive servicing since 1840 when the Eastern Counties Railway first established facilities and the main workshops were transferred to here in 1848. Steam locomotives were constructed here until the 1920s, while the depot had the largest steam loco allocation of any shed in the country. Stratford received its first allocation of diesels in 1958. Diesel servicing co-existed with steam until the latter ended in 1962. The former GER High Meade engine shop, constructed between 1914 and 1918, was converted as a heavy diesel repair facility in 1958–59. This repair shop (known as 'The Works') then became responsible for the Eastern Region's diesel allocation for the London and East Anglia area. As late as 1986 Stratford still had an allocation of seventy-nine main line locos and twenty-five shunters, but its importance as a diesel depot declined with the electrification of the main lines to Norwich and Kings Lynn and of the diesel worked branches. Later known as Stratford Level 5 depot, the Works closed from 31 March 1991. 2 July 2001 saw the end of an era with the closure of Stratford diesel depot, replaced from the same day by a new £11 million EWS diesel servicing facility, retaining the same name, but located at Temple Mills, Leyton. The old depot was due to be swept away as construction started on phase 2 of the Channel Tunnel Rail Link.

The construction work on the Channel Tunnel Rail Link started almost immediately in July when Transport Minister John Spellar ceremoniously launched a drilling rig to start the building of twin bore tunnels and an international passenger station. This was the culmination of a thirteen-year campaign for a station to be included at Stratford on the high-speed link. The CTRL from St Pancras opened on 14 November 2007, but Stratford International did not open until 30 November 2009. The new Stratford International

Station is some 400 metres away from the domestic station and is linked by an extension to the Docklands Light Railway.

In addition to the passenger lines and the railway works and maintenance depot, there were also extensive sidings for carriages. Freight facilities at Stratford included a Freightliner terminal and the London International Freight Terminal, both closed by 2006, while just to the north at Leyton was the vast Temple Mills hump marshalling yard built in the 1950s, but the cessation of wagon-load freight made it redundant, and the hump closed in 1982.

It was this vast extent of largely redundant land that made Stratford the ideal location for London's Olympic bid venue. With the successful award of the 2012 Olympic Games, Stratford station became of strategic importance and a massive total of £102.5 million was put aside for enhancements to increase capacity. Among this, new platforms were provided for the North London Link services, now operated as part of the London Overground. The North Woolwich line closed in 2006 as it was replaced by a new DLR line via London City Airport, later extended to Woolwich Arsenal; but the section from Canning Town to Stratford became another DLR line extended to the new Stratford International station.

Before Covid-19, Stratford was the busiest station on the Underground outside the Central Area Zone 1. However, in November 2021 the *Metro* newspaper reported that Stratford had overtaken Waterloo as Britain's busiest railway station, a title it had held for seventeen years. An estimated 14 million passengers travelled though Stratford in the year to 31 March according to the Office of Rail and Road. With the opening of the Elizabeth Line (aka Crossrail) in stages from 24 May 2022 the station has grown in importance as the Shenfield–Liverpool Street service, formerly run as part of TfL Rail, has become part of the new Elizabeth Line network. However, in 2023 Liverpool Street has replaced Stratford as Britain's busiest station.

This aerial view of Stratford in 1991 shows the extent of land taken up by the railways at that time with the station at the bottom right and the diesel depot and freight terminals in the middle. (M. Batten collection)

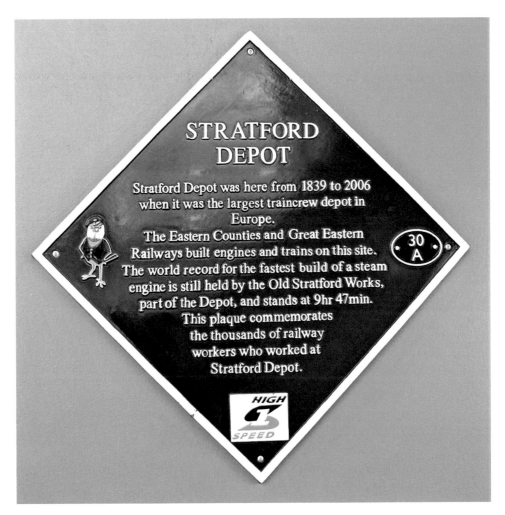

This plaque mounted inside the concourse of Stratford International station commemorates the locomotive depot that previously occupied the site.

DID YOU KNOW?
In 1891 the Stratford Railway Works of the Great Eastern Railway fully erected a locomotive in 9 hours, 47 minutes – a world record never beaten.

The Stratford–North Woolwich Line

The first section of a line south from Stratford was opened by the Eastern Counties & Thames Junction Railway in 1846 to bring seaborne coal traffic from the River Thames near Bow Creek. The line was extended to North Woolwich, opened on 14 June 1847 and was soon after purchased by the Eastern Counties Railway. A railway-owned ferry service ran from here to Woolwich on the south bank, although this ceased after the London County Council started a free ferry over the same route in 1889.

The opening of the Royal Victoria Dock (1855) Royal Albert Dock (1880) and King George V Dock (1921) brought new traffic to the line but also required some alterations to the route including a tunnel at Silvertown. The original routeing was retained for freight, later being known as the Silvertown tramway. The Port of London Authority had its own complex of railway lines serving the Royal Docks until these closed in May 1970.

Branches came off the line at Custom House for Beckton and its gasworks (1874) and Gallions (1880), but these lost their passenger services in 1940 following air-raid damage. Through trains from North Woolwich to London via the southern curve at Stratford also ceased in October 1940, trains then running to Palace Gates until 1963 and Stratford thereafter.

By the 1970s the North Woolwich line was in serious decline. However, salvation for the line came with the electrification of the line and linking it to the North London Line.

The electric trains did not operate into the 1854 North Woolwich station however, because a new station alongside had opened in 1979. The former station, a listed building was converted to become a railway museum. This opened in 1984 and was run by Newham Council but was later run down and closed in 2008.

Following privatisation the line passed to North London Railways, who subsequently rebranded themselves as Silverlink. Silvertown station was rebuilt in the late 1980s and renamed Silvertown & London City Airport. However, as it did not actually connect with the airport, a new Docklands Light Railway line from Canning Town to King George V via London City Airport opened on 2 December 2005. This was extended to Woolwich Arsenal in 2009. The Silverlink service was withdrawn between Stratford and North Woolwich in December 2006 as this largely paralleled the route. Part of the line passed to the DLR as mentioned earlier, and another section has become part of the Elizabeth Line.

North Woolwich station in March 2022. After years of neglect, it has recently gained a new tenant and been repainted externally.

Part of the display inside the station when it was in use as a museum.

This landscaped patch of land between two roads is the former trackbed of the line into North Woolwich. Beyond the wall and gate is where the Elizabeth Line descends into tunnel to cross under the Thames and through to Woolwich and Abbey Wood.

Docklands Light Railway

With the closure of the docks and their redevelopment by the London Docklands Development Corporation (see chapter 4) the LDDC saw a rail-based system as the key to attracting up to 9,000 jobs to the area. Adopting a light rail system would be cheaper than an extension of the Underground and had the advantage of being able to utilise some existing but redundant infrastructure.

The original routes were from Tower Gateway to Island Gardens, from where a foot tunnel gives access to Greenwich on the south bank; and from Stratford to Island Gardens, the lines joining at West India Quay. At Stratford trains used the previously unadopted platform 4.

The railway was formally opened by Elizabeth II on 30 July 1987 and opened to the public a month later. The main area around Canary Wharf was yet to be redeveloped so trains stopped at a temporary location in the middle of a building site (without the doors opening).

The DLR as built had several key innovations. The trains, twin-car articulated sets carried no driver, being controlled by automatic train operation. The stations were of modular design and unstaffed, all ticketing being by machines. All stations were built to be fully wheelchair accessible and with straight platforms.

As the area developed, it was soon obvious that extensions and enhancements would be needed. Olympia & York, developers of Canary Wharf, wanted direct access to the City of London and so put forward a private capital grant towards an extension. This opened fully in November 1991.

A second line from Poplar to Beckton opened on 28 March 1994. To accommodate the growing demand now that the Canary Wharf area had been redeveloped, trains were extended to two units. A new main depot was built at Beckton, on the site of the former gas works.

Further extensions have created an extension from Island Gardens to Lewisham and new lines from Canning Town to Woolwich Arsenal via London City Airport and from Canning Town to Stratford International. It now serves forty-five stations with 149 trains and in 2017 average daily usage was some 340,000 according to DfT figures.

London Tilbury & Southend Railway

Another railway, the London, Tilbury & Southend (LT&SR), also served Newham. The LT&SR was the chief rival to the Great Eastern within East London and Essex, having an alternative route to the popular seaside town of Southend and serving Tilbury Docks, which first opened in 1886. Local services between Bromley-by-Bow and Barking were transferred to extend the District Railway (now District Line) in 1908. Much to the GER's annoyance, the LT&SR sold out to the Midland Railway rather than the GER in 1912. Thus, the line became part of the LMS rather than the LNER at the 1923 Grouping; and in turn passed to the BR Midland Region at Nationalisation. However, in 1949 it was transferred to Eastern Region control. Now it operates separate from TfL or Greater Anglia as the c2c franchise and certain trains run via Stratford to Liverpool Street.

Robert

Steam locomotive *Robert* is plinthed on a length of track outside Stratford station. However, despite Stratford's history as a railway works, this locomotive has no connection with Stratford or indeed Newham. *Robert* is a 1933 0-6-0ST built by Avonside of Bristol which worked at an ironstone mine in Northamptonshire. It was bought by the London Docklands Development Corporation and originally displayed at the site of Beckton Gas Works. It passed to the London Borough of Newham in 2000 and moved to Stratford until 2008. It was removed while construction work for the Olympics took place at Stratford, returning newly repainted to its present position outside the station in 2011.

Robert at its present location outside Stratford station.

Buses Trams and Trolleybuses

Between 1829 and 1836 engineer Walter Hancock (1799–1852) built a number of successful steam-powered omnibuses in Stratford. One of these, the ten-seat *Infant* of 1829 ran services between Stratford and central London in 1831 and even ran a trip to Brighton in 1832. The later *Enterprise* (1833) began running a regular service between London Wall and Paddington, while the twenty-two-seat *Automaton* (1836) also ran on this route and between Moorgate and Stratford reaching speeds of up to 15 mph. However, heavy road tolls and speed limits imposed by the Turnpike Acts caused him to cease running and horse power would remain until the electric trams and petrol motor buses took over in the next century.

Both East Ham and West Ham Corporations had their own tram fleets, as did also the London County Council, Barking, Ilford and Walthamstow boroughs. Their fleets all passed to London Transport on its formation in 1933. Some were to remain in use until the end of London's tramways in 1952. Former West Ham four-wheel tram No. 102 was preserved in its later guise as London Transport 290. One of six built in 1910 and later rebuilt, they were withdrawn in 1937/38 as a result of trolleybuses being introduced, but 290 was saved by London Transport for preservation. This is now housed at the London Transport Museum, Covent Garden, and has been repainted into its original identity as West Ham 102.

East Ham's tram depot was built as part of the Town Hall complex. After its demise as a tram depot it was used to house council vehicles. Part of the building in Nelson Street, East Ham, is seen here.

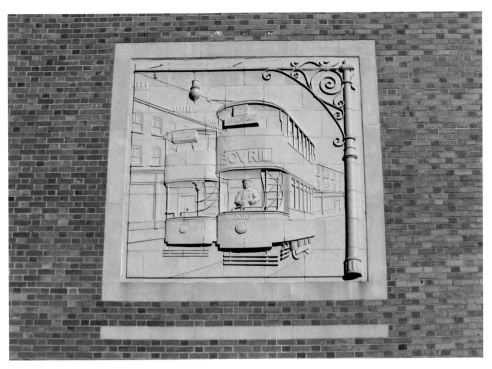

This wall plaque is mounted on the building to mark the location of the former East Ham Council tramways depot.

West Ham Corporation Tramways officially started on 27 February 1904. The Corporation opened their new tram depot in Greengate Street on 25 October 1906, replacing former temporary premises. The depot had accommodation for some ninety trams, workshops, and offices. Unusually there was also a recreation room complete with a piano. The site had space to extend the shed to take a further forty trams for future expansion.

In 1936 work began on converting the site for trolleybuses to replace trams. In fact, a pioneer trolleybus had been demonstrated in Greengate Street back in 1912, only a year after the first trolleybuses had been introduced to Britain in Leeds and Bradford. Trolleybuses started working from West Ham on 6 June 1937. The last trams from the depot ceased on 8 June 1940 and these were the last trams to serve Newham. The final London Transport trams would cease in 1952.

Conversion to buses started in 1959 when fifteen Routemasters entered service from West Ham. The final trolleybuses went on 26 April 1960. The official last trolleybus was No. 622 which had inaugurated the services in 1937. Another bus garage, Forest Gate, in Green Street, Upton Park, dating from 1898, was closed at the same time and its allocation transferred to West Ham. There was capacity for 186 buses, but the allocation declined in later years. In February 1987 the allocation was down to 113. The garage was closed in 1992. A new housing development was built on the site by 1996 and the access road for this was named Routemaster Close.

The surviving offices of West Ham bus garage.

A war memorial is sited outside the bus garage commemorating the employees who lost their lives fighting in the First World War.

Routemaster Close. The road sign is a reminder of the former bus garage and the classic London Transport Routemaster buses that worked from there.

In Upton Park at the end of Priory Road was Upton Park bus garage. This was originally opened in 1907 for motorbuses by the London Road Car Company. A year later they merged with the London General Omnibus Company. In 1931 the garage was rebuilt and extended. As such it was claimed as the largest LGOC garage with an area of 71,000 square feet and an allocation of over 200 buses. The garage passed to London Transport on its formation in 1933 and still had an allocation of over 200 buses in 1952. However, a combination of industrial and population decline and increasing car ownership saw a reduction in bus services and the allocation had fallen to 108 by November 1976 and eighty-nine in February 1987. The garage was closed in September 2011.

Following the privatisation of London Buses in the 1990s, new companies Stagecoach and First Bus had opened garages in Waterden Road, Stratford. However, these had to close in 2008 as they came within the area they would be redeveloped as the Olympic Games site. A new site was found by the Olympic Delivery Authority for Stagecoach near West Ham station on land used formerly by Parcelforce.

DID YOU KNOW?
The road from Wanstead to North Woolwich (A116/A117) including High Street North and South, East Ham was designated part of the North Circular Road, until the South Woodford to Barking relief road (A406) was built in the 1980s. There was extensive lorry traffic heading to and from the docks.

4. Docks and Shipping

The Royal Docks

London's docks grew in a piecemeal pattern. By the end of the eighteenth century, the riverbank around the Tower of London was crowded with wharves and warehouses, while the tidal river was congested with shipping trying to reach them. Smuggling and theft were rife. The solution was to build enclosed docks with a permanent water level controlled by lock gates. The first commercial dock to be opened, by the West India Dock Company in 1802, was on the Isle of Dogs. Four years later a second dock was added, and the East India Dock Company opened its own dock at Blackwall. Others followed, for example London Docks (1805), and St Katharine Dock (1828) on the north bank; and what were to become known as the Surrey Commercial Docks on the south side.

These were all designed for sailing ships and built before the advent of railways. The opening of the railway line to North Woolwich prompted the building of the Victoria (later Royal Victoria) Dock, opened in 1855. This was the first to be designed specifically for steamships and to have rail access. This was followed by Millwall Docks in 1868. The Royal Albert Dock opened in 1880 at the southern end of East Ham parish, built on marshland east of the Royal Victoria Dock, with direct access eastward to the Thames at Gallions Reach; and the first development at Tilbury, 22 nautical miles downriver, opened in 1886.

By the end of the nineteenth century, London had already become the world's leading port. It handled more cargo by both weight and value than any other UK port. But the various docks were owned by a number of companies who competed not only with each other, but also with the private riverside wharves, and they were losing money. The 'Free Water Clause' gave lightermen free access to the enclosed docks. It was estimated that by 1900 over 80 per cent of all imports handled in the enclosed docks was being discharged to lighters for onward carriage to private wharves, earning the dock companies no revenue on this cargo.

A Royal Commission was set up in 1900 and published its findings in 1902. It recommended a single, unified public authority to run the docks, act in the interests of all port users and provide whatever navigational facilities were considered necessary. The government accepted the findings and placed a bill before Parliament in 1903. This finally became law on 21 December 1908, and thus the Port of London Authority came into being in 1909.

In 1921 the 'Royal' group of docks was completed with the opening of the King George V Dock by His Majesty on 8 July. Between them, the Royal Docks comprised the largest area of impounded dock water in the world, with over 11 miles of quays. A dry dock 750 feet long by 100 feet wide was provided at King George V Dock complementing two other dry docks in the Royal Albert Dock. The docks had rail connections to the main lines, the PLA having their own internal fleet of dock shunting locomotives until railway operations ceased in 1970.

London's docks were to suffer severe damage in the Blitz, especially on the night of 7 September 1940. But they recovered and were rebuilt during the 1950s, although imports now far exceeded exports.

The docks reached their highest point of activity in 1964 when trade exceeded 61 million tons, but change was soon to come. The introduction of new cargo handling methods with containerisation and roll-on, roll-off ferries made the old docks redundant as they were not suited to the quick turn-rounds of the new technologies, nor could some of them handle the larger ships being built. New facilities were developed at Tilbury and the older docks gradually closed. The smaller, older docks closed first in 1967–68. Finally, the Royals closed commercially in 1981, although some ships remained laid up there until 1985. After that all activity was concentrated at Tilbury.

The closure of the docks led to their redevelopment by the London Docklands Development Corporation. At the 'Royals' a new campus of the University of East London and the London City Airport now occupy the area, as well as the Excel Exhibition Centre and the Crystal Building – now the new home for the London Assembly. The docks themselves were not filled in. Maritime access is still maintained to West India Dock – often used by vessels on courtesy visits, and to the 'Royals' – used for events at Excel such as the former London International Boat Show. During the London Olympic Games in 2012 two cruise ships were moored in Royal Albert Dock to provide accommodation for the hundreds of bus drivers brought in from all over the country to drive buses on park & ride services and to transport the 'Games Family' – athletes, media, sponsors, etc., between venues.

Most warehouses and other dock buildings have gone but some warehouses remain at Royal Victoria Dock and are used in conjunction with the Excel Exhibition Centre; however, other remnants of the former use can be found if you know where to look.

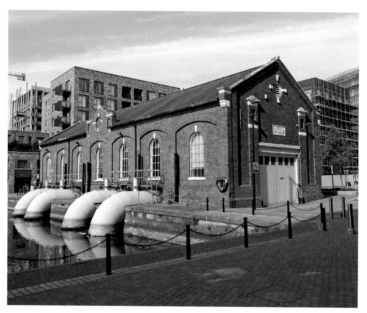

This former PLA pumphouse alongside the eastern lock entrance to the Royal Albert Dock is dated 1912 and was used to regulate the water level within the dock. Similar buildings survive elsewhere at St Katharine Dock and West India Dock.

Spiller's Millennium Mill, Royal Victoria Dock, viewed from the DLR Pontoon Dock station. This was built in 1905 for William Vernon & Sons, who were taken over by Spiller's in 1920. It was rebuilt following wartime damage but closed down along with the docks. New development plans were announced in 2022 and are now ongoing. The D silo nearby is Grade II listed.

The former bascule bridge on Woolwich Manor Way seen in 1977. The bridge was built by Sir William Arrol & Co. Ltd of Glasgow and was hydraulically powered. Buses on route 101 Wanstead–North Woolwich would often be held here as the bridge was lifted for ships to enter and leave the docks, giving upstairs passengers a grandstand view but a long wait. This bridge has been replaced by a modern electrically powered one, but the brick wall and pillars survive.

DID YOU KNOW?
On 6 August 1939 the Cunard-White Star liner SS *Mauritania* entered King George V Dock after its maiden Atlantic crossing. At 772 feet long and 89 feet 6 inches wide, it only just fitted into the entrance lock, which is 800 feet long and 100 feet wide. Over 100,000 people came to watch its entrance – the largest ship to ever enter the Royal Docks.

The Connaught Road swing bridge separates Royal Albert and Royal Victoria docks. A modern bridge is in place now, but this support for the former hydraulically worked bridge is preserved nearby. The old bridge carried a narrow road and also a railway line.

42

This statue, entitled *Landed* by Australian sculptor Les Johnson, was unveiled in Royal Victoria Square near the Excel Centre on 24 August 2009. It features three actual dockworkers – Johnny Ringwood, Mark Tibbs and Patrick Holland – and is dedicated to all the dock workers and their families. Johnny Ringwood and Patricia Holland, whose father and husband both worked on the docks, campaigned to raise the funds to create this statue.

Close by the access pier for the Woolwich ferry at North Woolwich is a small garden/seating area. Sited here are some old anchors and this hand crane.

Ship Repair

An adjunct to the docks was shipbuilding and the ship repair industry. Newham had two major companies engaged in this, Harland & Wolff Ltd and R. H. Green & Silley Wier. Harland & Wolff opened their works alongside the lock entrance to the King George V Dock in 1924. The works closed in 1972 and was later demolished. The site remained vacant for many years until a housing estate was constructed from 1999. The works of R. H. Green & Silley Wier on the south side of Royal Albert Dock have now been replaced by part of London City Airport.

The Harland & Wolff ship repair works alongside lock entrance to the King George V Dock. Ben Line's *Benledi* (1954, 8,800 grt) is entering the lock with Port of London Authority tug *Plangent* in attendance. (Photo courtesy of Reg Batten)

The gates from the entrance to Harland & Wolff are preserved in Lyle Park, Silvertown.

44

In Royal Victoria Park, North Woolwich, is a reminder of the latter company in the form of this steam hammer from the blacksmith's shop at their works.

Thames Ironworks

Thames Ironworks Ship Building & Engineering Company Ltd was one of the last large shipbuilding works on the Thames. It was situated in Bow Creek close to Canning Town station and started as C. J. Mare & Co. in 1846. Their production included a number of warships, of which one, HMS *Warrior*, survives and is preserved at Portsmouth Harbour. This is historically significant as Britain's first iron-hulled armoured warship, launched in 1860 at a cost of £377,292, and spans an interim period of development having both sails and steam propulsion. The last major warship built by the yard was HMS *Thunderer* in 1911. The following year Thames Ironworks declared bankruptcy and closed down as it was unable to compete with cheaper yards on Tyneside.

A major disaster occurred in June 1898, when HMS *Albion* was launched from the Thames Ironworks shipyards. A vast crowd, estimated at 30,000, came to witness the launching of the cruiser by the Duke and Duchess of York (later King George V and Queen Mary). Two hundred of the onlookers crowded onto a flimsy wooden walkway to get a better view. Unfortunately, when the ship was launched it caused a large wave, which washed away the supports of the walkway and threw all 200 into the 10-foot-deep water amid the debris. Rescuers saved about 160, but thirty-eight people were drowned.

The company had a works football team, who first played in 1895. This developed into the professional team West Ham United who established a stadium at the Boleyn Ground, Upton Park. The club's badge features a pair of crossed hammers and their nickname is 'The Hammers' or 'The Irons', reflecting on both their location and ancestry.

A memorial to the Thames Ironworks has been created in the stairwell to the new Canning Town station.

Part of the memorial to Thames Ironworks at Canning Town station.

The *Albion* memorial in East London Cemetery, Grange Road. This monument marks the grave of twenty-eight of the thirty-eight victims who died.

The *Albion* disaster, bad though it was, paled into insignificance compared to Newham's (and the Thames) worst marine disaster. The paddle steamer *Princess Alice* sank after a collision with collier *Bywell Castle* in Gallions Reach on 3 September 1878. It happened just after raw sewage had been released into the Thames from Beckton Sewage Works. Around 640 people were discovered drowned but there may have been more – no passenger list had been made. One consequence of this was that sewage was then shipped out to sea for dumping until 1998 when the practice was banned. A memorial was erected in Woolwich Cemetery where many of the dead were buried.

Facilities for Sailors and Passengers

Any docks area will also have had buildings erected to serve the needs of sailors and, where passengers were carried, to serve their needs.

Since Victorian times, West Ham has had a Black and Asian seamen's community around the docks. Indeed, in the 1930s Canning Town and Custom House had the largest Black population in London. In 1926 a Ceylonese-born minister, Pastor Kamal Chunchie, who had converted from Islam to Christianity, opened the Coloured Men's Institute in Tidal Basin Road as a social and support centre, having seen and experienced racism against the Black and Asian community. The institute provided food and accommodation, gave out food and clothing parcels to poor families, organised Christmas dinners and gifts and organised days out to the seaside. However, after only five years the institute was demolished for the construction of a new road to the docks, Silvertown Way.

The imposing Flying Angel hostel at Custom House was opened by the Missions to Seamen in 1936. It replaced an earlier establishment, the Louisa Ashburton House, erected by the British & Foreign Sailors Society, which had been demolished in 1930. The eight-storey Flying Angel building contained hostel accommodation, public rooms and a chapel. The Asiatic Hostel opened in the adjacent Ashburton Hall in 1937 to provide facilities for Indian seamen. Both buildings received war damage during the Blitz, and the Asiatic Hostel was later demolished. The Flying Angel closed as a seamen's hostel in 1973. It was later owned by Beacon hostels but is now converted to flats.

Right: The former Flying Angel hostel at Custom House.

Below: The Flying Angel motif over the entrance. On the roof is a weathervane in the form of a four-masted sailing ship.

The Fox Connaught pub, situated on the corner where Victoria Dock Road meets Connaught Bridge. The building was originally the Connaught Tavern and in 1881, when it was built, it catered for sea travellers via the docks. It was later a regular congregating point for dock labourers waiting for the 'call' to see if they would get a day's work.

The Gallions Hotel in Albert Basin Way, E16, was built in 1881–83 by the London & St Katharine Dock Company as the New Hotel to serve passengers boarding liners from the Royal Albert Dock. It was designed by George Vigers and T. R. Wagstaffe. There was a Gallions station on a branch off the line to North Woolwich, but this closed in 1940 following bomb damage. The hotel closed in 1972 and was then left derelict for many years, suffering from vandalism. Planning permission to move it to another site was sought in 1989 but this did not happen, and the hotel has since been renovated and renamed Galyons.

Woolwich Ferry and Tunnel

After the Great Eastern Railway line to North Woolwich opened in 1847 they commenced a railway-owned ferry service to Woolwich, although this ceased in 1908 after the London County Council started a free ferry over the same route in March 1889. The railway pier remained, being used by steamers plying between London and Gravesend or Southend and by locally based tugs but is now disused.

The free ferry for pedestrians and vehicles was initiated by the Metropolitan Board of Works who had been replaced by the London County Council by the time the ferry started. Three diesel ferries were built in 1963 to replace the four previous paddle steamers. New loading piers opened in 1966 to provide 'drive-on, drive off' loading rather than the previous side loading system. The ferries were named after local politicians, Ernest Bevin, John Burns and James Newman. Two new ferries were built in 2018 and entered service from February 2019. These were built in Poland and are diesel-electric hybrid vessels.

This view shows the remains of the old railway pier. Beyond this is the loading pier for the ferry with one of the two current ferries tied up alongside.

The Woolwich foot tunnel was opened in October 1912, having been constructed at a cost of £87,000. It is 1,665 feet in length, lined with white tiles. The entrance shafts have a spiral staircase and a lift, previously manually operated. That on the north bank descends 64 feet; on the south bank it is 51 feet. The tunnel roof is 38 feet below the water surface level at low tide and 69 feet at high tide.

DID YOU KNOW?
The names of the two new Woolwich ferries which entered service in 2019 are *Dame Vera Lynn*, the legendary singer born in East Ham, and *Ben Woollacott*, a nineteen-year-old deckhand who drowned after being dragged overboard while working on the ferries.

5. Housing

Although much of the industrial development in East and West Ham and the accompanying housing for workers dated from the second half of the nineteenth century, there were a number of more gentrified properties in the Plaistow and Upton areas from the previous century or earlier, built as the country retreats for City merchants and businessmen. However, most of these have not survived. For instance, Ham House originated in the sixteenth century as Grove House, later known as Rookes Hall and later still as Ham House. In the eighteenth century the eminent surgeon Dr John Fothergill turned the site into one of the finest botanical gardens in Europe. Ham House was demolished in 1872. At that time it was owned by the Gurney family who sold the land in 1874 for use as a park – now West Ham Park. Central Park, East Ham and Stratford Park are also on the grounds of former large estates. Upton House in Upton Lane was the birthplace of Lord Joseph Lister (1827–1912), the founder of antiseptic surgery. The house was demolished in 1968. Cumberland House stood in Elkington Road off New Barn Street. It took its name from the Duke of Cumberland, George III's younger brother, who owned the house between 1787 and 1790. This was demolished in 1935.

When industry first came to Canning Town and Silvertown, new houses were built to house the workers, but these were often poorly built without gas supply and with open sewers. In 1855 Albert Dickens, brother of the author Charles Dickens, published a Board of Health report about the area, stating: 'It was impossible to describe the miserable state Canning Town was in: there was neither drainage nor paving; in Winter the streets were impassable; the cholera raged very much in this district.'

The vast rows of late nineteenth-century terraced houses may seem at first glance to be similar in design, but a more careful examination will show that there are often several different batches of similar houses in a street. A builder would build a small terrace of houses for rent, perhaps occupying one himself, and maybe creating a yard for maintenance. Then another builder would erect another terrace further along the road to a slightly different design. The builders could buy pre-made standard components such as lintels, windowsills and decorative mouldings. These terraced houses would be rented to clerks, shop assistants, small tradesmen etc and there would often be multiple occupancy.

The coming of the railways encouraged the growth of commuting to work in London, and there were also larger detached and semi-detached houses aimed at the better-off commuter. In 1877 the MP and philanthropist Thomas Corbett and his son Archibald started the Woodgrange estate in Forest Gate. Over the next fifteen years they built over 1,100 houses which were sold on ninety-nine-year leases. There was an overall design theme although with some variations and there were regulations about how the houses should be decorated externally. Some came with glazed canopies at the front and many had servants' quarters alongside.

Along the south side of Romford Road in Forest Gate are a group of three pairs of small cottages, which seem older and out of keeping with the Victorian and Edwardian surroundings. These were built as farm cottages in 1840 and give a glimpse of the area's rural past.

A lot of houses were destroyed during the Second World War, so there was a large programme of council housing construction in the 1950s and 1960s, also incorporating a degree of slum clearance. The first tower blocks in the area were built at Canning Town in 1961.

The boost to the area created in the aftermath of the Olympic Games has seen another massive surge in property development, much of it in high-rise apartments, particularly around the Olympic Park site at Stratford but also around Canning Town and Silvertown.

Cyprus Estate

The Cyprus housing estate for the workers of Royal Albert Dock (opened in 1880), Cyprus Place, was built on the north side of the dock. The streets were named after people and places in the news during the previous decade, e.g. the explorers Stanley and Livingstone and Prime Minister Lord Beaconsfield. The British had taken over the administration of Cyprus from Turkey in 1878.

The docks were badly bombed in the war and much of the housing at Cyprus was lost and replaced after the war by 'pre-fabs'. With the economic desolation of the Docklands in the 1980s, Cyprus was the location of the first new private housing development in the area for many years, and the first sponsored by the London Docklands Development Corporation.

Since 1994 Cyprus is also the name of an adjacent station on the Docklands Light Railway, the nearest station for the University of East London Docklands Campus.

The former Ferndale Hotel public house on the corner of Ferndale Street and Cyprus Place, now private housing, is the only remaining building from the former estate.

Woolwich Borough Council built these 'Working Class Dwellings' in Bargehouse Road, North Woolwich, in 1901. There is a plaque below the roof, but the writing is no longer legible. There also used to be a wooden sign on the end wall that said 'To Ferry and Railway Station' but that disappeared shortly after the station closed in 2006. On the opposite side of the road is a more modern set of terraced houses, built in a style that mimics and complements the original dwellings.

The Keir Hardie Estate at Canning Town was built in 1947 as part of the post-war rebuilding programme. It became a model for council estate building elsewhere in Britain.

54

Ronan Point

Ronan Point was a twenty-two-storey tower block on Butchers Road, Custom House. On the morning of 16 May 1968, only two months after opening, a gas explosion occurred in one of the flats on the eighteenth floor. This blew out some load-bearing walls, causing a whole corner of the block to collapse. Four people were killed and thirteen injured. This and the other similar blocks nearby were refurbished but all were later torn down and replaced by houses in 1986.

As a result of this, there was a backlash against high-rise blocks of flats for several years until the extent of the housing shortfall in London, and the lack of available land for building, sparked a revival. The investigation into the causes of the explosion led to changes and new guidelines in the construction of tower blocks.

Ronan Point showing the devastation caused by the explosion. (Photo courtesy of Newham Archives, Newham Heritage Service)

6. Behind the Façade: Repurposed Buildings

Over the years many buildings that have been erected have ceased to be used for their original purpose. Industries close down or moved away. Amenities like cinemas closed as leisure habits changed with emerging technologies. Many of the area's public houses have closed as the now majority Muslim population do not fraternise them. Some buildings get demolished and replaced but others remain, though now with an alternative use.

Trebor Sweets
There is no mistaking the origins of this one! In 1907 Messrs Robertson and Woodcock opened a sweets factory in Shaftesbury Road, Forest Gate. It was built around a row of pre-existing houses called Trebor Terrace, off Katherine Road, and hence the name was adopted in 1918. A new factory, in contemporary modernist style was built on the site in 1935. Later expansion saw them take over an old coach factory in Woodford. By the 1960s Trebor claimed to be the UK's largest confectionary maker and exported to over fifty countries. However, in 1989 they were taken over by Cadbury's and the factory closed down. The 1935 factory survives, little altered externally but now converted to residential apartments.

Externally, the former Trebor Sweets factory still looks much as it did in its commercial days.

Church Road Studios in Church Road, Manor Park, houses a number of community organisations, including the Shade Centre. The building was originally a laundry. In the days before people had washing machines and before launderettes (introduced from 1949) laundering clothes was a laborious task that took housewives a considerable time to do by hand washing and then putting the clothes through a mangle to remove most of the water before hanging them up to dry. Larger items like sheets and blankets could be sent to laundries like this, whose vans would collect and return the items.

Quadrangle House, Stratford, E15. This imposing block, now converted to apartment flats, was formerly offices of the London Electricity Board, who were responsible for the supply of electricity and retail of electrical appliances throughout the London area from nationalisation in 1948 until privatised in 1990.

Newham has lost many of its public houses as the now majority Muslim population does not drink alcohol. Many of these have been repurposed but their distinct architectural style can be an identifier to their origins. This flamboyantly styled example in Katherine Road is now a Paddy Power betting shop.

Perhaps even more imposing was the Earl of Essex on the corner of High Street North and Romford Road, Manor Park. A plaque reveals that this was built in 1902 and that the architects were Henry Poston and W. E. Trent while the builder was W. J. Maddison. Closed for many years, this was used for a while after closure as low-cost housing. In 2023 this was undergoing refurbishment.

Next door to the Earl of Essex was the Coronation cinema. Like all the other former cinemas in Newham, this has closed as a cinema and is now the Royal Regency banqueting suite. The former name can still be seen at roof level.

Of a more modern design, the former Boleyn Cinema in Barking Road also still bears its former name, but as can be seen it is now home to the International Gospel of Truth Church. It is bordered on both sides by a 'Magazin Romanesc' or Romanian shop. This was demolished in 2023 for a new housing development.

A building in Earlham Grove, Forest Gate, is now The Cherubim & Seraphim Church, an African church originating in Nigeria, but was previously Earlham Hall, a music college. John Curwen (1816–80) popularised the 'Tonic Sol-Fa' form of musical notation and established this college to teach it. He also set up the Tonic Sol-Fa Press in North Street, Plaistow (later the Curwen Press). He was also minister at Plaistow Congregationalist Church, Balaam Street from 1844 to 1864. His son founded the Stratford and East London Music Festival.

The street names Earlham Grove and nearby Sprowston Road are reminders of the famous Quaker banking family the Gurneys. They lived at Earlham Hall and Sprowston Hall in Norfolk. Samuel Gurney bought Ham House in Upton in 1812 and rebuilt the Cedars on adjoining land for his sister, the prison reformer Elizabeth Fry, who lived there from 1829 to 1844.

The former Earlham Hall music college in Earlham Grove, now a church.

This impressive-looking five-storey building in Greengate Street was built in 1921 for the Young Men's Christian Association (YMCA) as a club. It later became part of the Polytechnic of East London. This in turn was redesignated as the University of East London in 1992. With the opening of the new campus in Docklands in 1999 this site became redundant and was sold off for conversion to flats. The exterior remains largely original.

The style of the roof logo and lettering gave rise to its name as the Red Triangle Club.

Above: This somewhat anonymous building in Stratford High Street houses a restaurant, but once had a far more illustrious purpose. Opened in 1896 and designed by Frank Matcham, this was the former Borough Theatre. It was the largest theatre in Essex, seating over 3,000. Famous performers there included Ellen Terry, Sir Henry Irving and Beerbohm Tree, who opened it. In 1933 the theatre was converted to become the Rex Cinema, but this closed in 1969 and it became a bingo hall for a while.

Right: Not visible from street level but evident from across the road (or from the top deck of a bus) is the lettering 'Borough Theatre'. A bust of Beethoven also adorns the frontage.

7. Newham in the Two World Wars

When the First World War broke out, many people thought it would be all over in a few months. But it would go on to be one of longest and deadliest conflicts in history. Men voluntarily signed up at first and were later conscripted from 1916.

Before the war there had been a large German community but now despite many having been settled in the UK for many years they were classed as 'Enemy Aliens' by the government and forced to report their movements to the police. There was a strong anti-German sentiment, which led to homes and shops belonging to Germans or those with Germanic-sounding names being attacked.

> DID YOU KNOW?
> A public house on the south side of Stratford Broadway used to be named The King of Prussia, commemorating Frederick the Great (1740–86). However, in 1914 with the outbreak of the First World War it was patriotically renamed King Edward VII, a name it still carries.

The Silvertown Explosion

West Ham came through the First World War relatively unscathed (unlike what was to happen the second time around). In fact, the biggest disaster to strike the area could be said to be self-inflicted. This was the Silvertown Disaster of 1917.

One of the main industries in Silvertown was the Brunner Mond chemical factory, which produced soda crystals and caustic soda. However, the caustic soda plant had been closed down in 1912 and was standing idle. In 1915, this was 'practically requisitioned' by the government agency of the Explosives Supply Department, who wanted to use it to purify the explosive trinitrotoluene (TNT) for use in ammunition. This was despite the fact that the plant was located in a heavily populated area, which also had other volatile chemical and refining industries, a point stressed by the Brunner Mond directors who were opposed to the plans. The government thought that the production of TNT was safe as long as the purification process (to be undertaken here) was kept separate from the manufacture of raw TNT. Consequently, the processes did not have to comply with the regulations of the 1875 Explosives Act.

Production started in September 1915 on a twenty-four-hour basis, employing three shifts. The protracted battles of trench warfare were consuming vast quantities of ammunition (and lives), while making little tactical advance. Raw TNT was delivered in sacks or barrels and hoisted to a room above the melt pot. Then about 5 tons at a time was poured down into the melt pot, which was heated by steam coils. The molten TNT ran into one of four vertical cylinders, where it was dissolved in warm alcohol. When the solution was cooled, TNT was left behind as crystals, while most of the impurities were left in the alcohol solution. The process was repeated until sufficiently purified. The pure TNT was packed into 50 lb cotton bags. Thus, the plant housed crude, partly refined and purified TNT. Elsewhere on the site, and kept separate from the TNT production, Bruner Mond continued to manufacture soda crystals.

Well on the night of Friday 19 January 1917, the inevitable happened and there was an explosion at 6.52 pm. It is believed that this was caused by a fire in the melt pot room. The reason for the fire breaking out was not established, as the witnesses who raised the alarm were killed in the explosion. Conspiracy theories started to appear soon after that it might have been that a German spy had sabotaged the plant. However, it should not have been unexpected though. Only in the previous month, the plant had been visited by a government inspector, whose report stated: 'It is perfectly clear that the management at Silvertown did not pay sufficient attention to the explosion risk attached to the handling of TNT.' In particular he reported that there were no precautions in place against friction sparks. The explosion was so severe that it destroyed the factory, other local factories, the local fire station (which was opposite the factory) and damaged thousands of homes. It was estimated some 60–70,000 properties received damage. Large red-hot lumps of metal were blown hundreds of yards to set off new fires where they landed. The explosion could be heard, and the shockwave felt all over London and Essex. It could even be heard in Norwich and Southampton, over 100 miles away, while the fires that followed could be seen from afar as Guildford and Maidstone.

Sixty-nine people were killed in the explosion with four more subsequently dying from their injuries. It could have been even more if it had happened earlier. Luckily many of the workers had already finished their shift and gone home. The explosion started fires that were to rage for nearly forty-eight hours and cause much more destruction. At the adjacent Silvertown Lubricants plant two oil tanks were torn apart and were ablaze. The Venesta plywood and packaging case works was destroyed. Two flour mills were ablaze, while a gasholder on the south side of the Thames was destroyed in a spectacular fireball.

As well as the casualties, another ninety-eight people were seriously injured and more than 900 suffered minor injuries.

Following the explosion, many local children who had been injured or traumatised were sent to the country to recuperate. A lot of these went to Parkwood near Maidstone, but others went elsewhere.

Some of the business properties damaged in the explosion were repaired by their owners an example being Lyle's sugar refinery. However, it was realised that the landlords of houses would probably not be able to afford the cost of repairs and so the government funded this. Houses were repaired rather than completely replaced. The first families were able to move back in by March. Landlords were not permitted to raise rents as a result of repairs being made.

You might think the explosion would have been seen as a national disaster and scandal, with calls for persons responsible to be brought to justice. But this was in the middle of a world war. Thousands of lives had already been lost in the conflict and many more would follow before peace eventually came. Furthermore, there was censorship in place on the post and printed news (there was no radio, TV, internet or social media back then). National newspapers did not give the location of the explosion, writing simply 'a munitions factory east of London'. There was a positive spin – 'munitions production will not be affected' – and praise for the courage of rescuers. However, there was some criticism of poor safety management. The Minister of Munitions visited the area on Saturday and the prime minister on Sunday.

The Silvertown explosion is commemorated locally by a memorial that was placed at the entrance to the former factory in North Woolwich Road. On 19 January 2017 the centenary of the Silvertown explosion was commemorated. Descendants of the families of those who died came to lay wreaths and remember the tragic event that took so many lives and caused so much destruction. The area has changed a lot in those 100 years, but the greatest changes have taken place recently. In 2017 the by now disused industrial sites that replaced the Brunner Mond plant and others destroyed at the time had been swept away and a vast new housing development of apartments and ancillary facilities was being constructed on the site, now renamed Royal Wharf. The memorial was relocated from its original site on the main road at the entrance to the former factory, where latterly it had been overshadowed by the viaduct of the Docklands Light Railway. It has been cleaned and re-sited on a grassed area within the new development.

There was another plaque outside the replacement Silvertown fire station to the firemen who lost their lives at the original station.

There is also a plaque in Postman's Park, in the City of London to policeman PC Greenoff. who stayed at his post outside the factory when the fire started to warn people of the danger. He was struck by debris from the explosion and died later from his injuries. He was awarded a posthumous King's Police Medal.

The memorial to the victims of the Silvertown explosion in its new location at Royal Wharf. This was photographed shortly after the centenary event in 2017.

Above: The fire station plaque in 2017. The station has since closed down.

Right: The firemen's grave in West Ham Cemetery.

Jack Cornwell VC

The naval war brought forth local victims and also heroes. Best remembered of these is John 'Jack' Travers Cornwell, killed in the battle of Jutland on 31 May 1916, aged just sixteen. He joined the Royal Navy in October 1915. Despite being badly wounded, and under heavy enemy gunfire, he maintained his post as part of the gun crew of HMS *Chester*. He died at Grimsby three days later. He was awarded a posthumous Victoria Cross and is buried in Manor Park Cemetery. The Manor Park branch of the Royal British Legion used to mount an annual parade around the ward in which he lived. Members of various Legion branches, plus sea and air cadets from the Cornwell VC Cadet Centre in Vicarage Lane, East Ham, attended, as did local dignitaries. A street and a tower block in Manor Park, where he lived, are named after him, as is a local public house. There also used to be a painting of him manning the gun displayed in Manor Park library.

Although Jack Cornwell is the most famous of Newham's First World War heroes, he was not the only local man to win the Victoria Cross. In fact, of a total of 634 people award the highest military honour during the conflict there were five who came from Newham. One who survived the war was Lance-Corporal Harold Sandford Mugford who lived in East Ham. Aged twenty-two, on 11 April 1917 during the battle for Arras in northern France, he was manning a machine gun when an enemy shell badly wounded him and broke both his legs. However, he remained firing his gun and urging others to take cover. He was brought back to England where both legs had to be amputated above the knee. He was presented with the VC by King George V in the grounds of Buckingham Palace on 3 July 1918. When he died in 1958 his funeral was attended by the mayors of East Ham and West Ham.

The other recipients of the Victoria Cross were Midshipman George Drewry, Captain Edgar Myles, and Second Lieutenant Bernard Cassidy. Midshipman Drewry from Forest Gate was in the Royal Naval Reserve and was just twenty when he won the award at Gallipoli in 1915 attempting to secure barges to act as a bridge for soldiers from his ship the SS *River Clyde* to reach the shore while under heavy enemy fire, and despite being wounded in the head by a shell fragment. He later reached the rank of lieutenant but was killed in an accident while on service in the Orkney Islands during 1918. He is buried in the City of London Cemetery.

DID YOU KNOW?
During the First World War a hostel for Belgian refugees fleeing the Germans was opened in Earlham Grove, Forest Gate.

In Memoriam

FIRST CLASS BOY JOHN TRAVERS
CORNWELL. V.C.
BORN 8th JANUARY 1900
DIED OF WOUNDS RECEIVED AT
THE BATTLE OF JUTLAND
2nd JUNE 1916.

THIS STONE WAS ERECTED
BY SCHOLARS AND EX-SCHOLARS
OF SCHOOLS IN EAST HAM.

"It is not wealth or ancestry
but honourable conduct and a noble
disposition that make men great." Ovid.

The grave of Jack Cornwell VC in Manor Park Cemetery.

Jack Cornwell 100

John (Jack) Travers Cornwell VC was born on the 8th January 1900. Jack joined the Royal Navy when he was just 15. On the 2nd May 1916 he joined the crew of HMS Chester this was just before the biggest sea battle of all time known as the Battle of Jutland which started on the 31st May. During the engagement, Jack as a Gunner Sight Setter was at his station when HMS Chester was attacked, and although he suffered serious wounds to his chest he remained at his post. Sadly, on the 2nd June 1916 in a Grimsby hospital Jack died.

On 15 September 1916, the official citation appeared in The London Gazette stating that John Travers Cornwell had been posthumously awarded the Victoria Cross by King George V.

The **Jack Cornwell 100** artwork has been produced as the result of collaboration with the Ladies of the Jack Cornwell Project: Jackie Beach, Jean Shea and Lesley Soloman, and professional artist Emma Barnard MA (RCA) to commemorate the 100th anniversary of Jack's life and death.

We would like to thank everyone who has supported this project.

The plaque at the community centre in Manor Park.

Community centre artwork produced to mark the centenary of his death.

The Second World War

When the Second World war started in 1939 over 16,000 children and expectant mothers were evacuated from East Ham and 32,000 from West Ham. But as no air raids came at first in the 'phoney war', children started to return to London. When the Blitz began in 1940 Newham came under heavy aerial bombardment from the Luftwaffe because of its strategic sites of the docks and railway yards. Over a quarter of West Ham's housing stock was destroyed and after the war the opportunity was taken to replace many of the poorer-quality slum housing areas that remained.

South Hallsville School

The Blitz started on Saturday 7 September 1940 – 'Black Saturday' – and would continue for fifty-seven days.

On the first day of the Blitz, 7 September, over 600 tons of explosives were dropped on the East End, with many people killed or injured. One of the streets to be hit was Martindale Road, Canning Town, just a hundred yards or so from the docks. At 5.55 a.m. on Sunday 8th, an unexploded high-explosive bomb was discovered at No. 8 in the road. Standard procedure in such cases was to evacuate all premises within a 600-yard radius until the bomb disposal people removed it – probably to Hackney Marshes where it could be safely detonated. Some people who had access to private transport, might choose to go to Essex or Kent. For everyone else though, and those made homeless by bomb damage it meant going to a designated rest centre from where they would be taken away by coach to places of greater safety. The local rest centre was at South Hallsville School. Ritchie Calder, a reporter from the *Daily Herald*, visited the school and found that arrangements were poorly organised. He felt that there was a disaster in the making if this should be hit and reported his concerns to the government.

There was more bombing on the evening of the 8th, and further families arrived at South Hallsville School. The school was becoming quite overcrowded and conditions inside were squalid, as electricity and water supplies had been cut off by the bombing. This situation continued into the next day. No coaches came to remove people. It was rumoured that coaches had been provided but had mistakenly been dispatched to Camden Town instead of Canning Town.

At around 4.30 a.m. on the 10th, news came through of a major incident at the school. It soon became clear that the school had received a direct hit causing massive casualties. It took days to sort through the debris, but eventually it was reported that seventy-three people had lost their lives in the explosion – most of them children. Of the dead, forty-four were residents of Martindale Road, evacuated because of the unexploded bomb. Bodies and body parts were taken to a temporary mortuary at West Ham Baths. It was not known how many people had been sheltering in the school, so it could not be ascertained if all had been accounted for. The journalist Ritchie Calder again visited the school after the bombing and reported on the failings of the authorities to plan for the social upheaval of people being bombed out of their homes.

Before the war the government had made extensive plans for potential gas attacks, issuing everyone with gas masks, and had supplied Anderson shelters for people with gardens that would provide some protection during air raids. But there was little provision for those made destitute and homeless through bombing. In 1941 Mr Calder wrote a book about his concerns, *The Lesson of London*.

There seemed to be an official prejudice against the poor. People were divided into 'natives' (those seeking help in their own areas) and 'immigrants' (those seeking help in another place, such as a neighbouring borough). Local authorities were supposed to deal with 'natives' and central government with 'immigrants'.

The Blitz continued for fifty-seven days. Over 5,000 people were killed and 25,000 made homeless. People started to seek shelter in the Underground stations. This was not allowed at first, but people just refused to leave and the authorities gave way. A Conservative MP Henry Willink was put in charge of dealing with the problems of rest centres and the homeless. He created one-stop information centres and produced a report, 'The Care of the Homeless'. Winston Churchill said that the homeless should be treated with kindness and generosity, but firmness. Henry Willink was later made Minister of Health and produced the first proposals for a National Health Service in 1944, which was introduced after the war.

The original school of 1878 was destroyed in the bombing and a new school later replaced it. Now it is known as Hallsville Primary School.

Another school to be destroyed by bombing was Upton Lane School, bult in 1894 and destroyed in 1944. The site was later used to build the new Stratford Grammar School in 1958.

Thousands of bombs, incendiaries, land mines, as well as V-1 'Doodlebug' and V-2 rockets, were dropped on Newham during the war. Some buildings were destroyed, others repaired. In some streets of terraced housing, a gap in the houses where more modern houses or flats have been built is a potential indication that the original premises were victims of such an attack.

On 18 September 1940 at approximately 9.30 p.m. a landmine explosion took out Nos 87–97 Third Avenue, Manor Park. Modern single-storey houses, set back from the road, have since been built where these once stood.

Among other buildings destroyed during the war were Queen's Cinema in Romford Road, Forest Gate, which was bombed in October 1941, and the Princess Alice public house on the corner of Romford Road and Woodgrange Road, bombed on 19 April 1941. This had been built in the 1860s and was named after one of Queen Victoria's daughters. It was later replaced by a new pub carrying the same name, but this closed down in 2007 and the building is now a Superdrug store.

War Memorials

Notable war memorials include those in Central Park, East Ham Cemetery, Abbey Road and the Samuel Gurney obelisk in Stratford Broadway, which are discussed in greater detail alongside their images here.

Other notable war memorials in Newham include that at the former West Ham bus garage (see p. 36), and one in the form of a plaque on the gates of Bridge Street Depot in Abbey Road. A memorial stands in the grounds of St Marks Church, Silvertown. At the Thames Barrier Park in Silvertown a memorial pavilion has been erected.

The war memorial in Central Park, East Ham, was unveiled in 1921. A total of 1,824 men are noted on the memorial. One of these is Frederick Gray, killed at Ypres on 2 May 1915. He was a member of the Second Battalion of the Essex Regiment, who were recruited from East and West Ham. The architect of the memorial was former East Ham mayor Mr Banks-Martin.

72

This war memorial in East Ham Cemetery commemorates all the war dead from the British Empire killed in the First World War. The cemetery also has a mass grave of people killed in the Blitz with a monument to them.

This war memorial in Abbey Road is not of municipal origin but was erected by the Crocketts' leather-cloth factory, which used to be sited here until 1961.

This memorial placed outside Forest Gate Police Station is a reminder that people from all walks of life enlisted during the First World War, and in many instances made the ultimate sacrifice.

8. Famous People and Memorials

Memorials

Samuel Gurney was the brother of prison reformer Elizabeth Fry and came from the prominent Quaker banking family. He lived in Stratford. In 1817 the pair campaigned to end capital punishment, which at the time was the punishment for a wide variety of crimes. They were unsuccessful but Elizabeth did succeed in her campaign for prison reform and Samuel was a leading figure in the fight to abolish slavery. After his death in 1856 the parishioners of West Ham paid for this obelisk in his memory.

Elizabeth Fry (1780–1845) lived for a time at a house, since demolished, in Portway, Stratford.

The Samuel Gurney obelisk in Stratford Broadway. The lettering on the plaque reads: 'In remembrance of Samuel Gurney who died the 5th of June 1856. Erected by his fellow parishioners and friends 1861. When the ear heard him then it blessed him.'

75

Outside Stratford library in The Grove is this memorial to Edith Kerrison (1850–1934), who was the first woman to serve on West Ham Council. The lettering reads: 'Erected by many friends in memory of a lifetime of service to others.' In front of this memorial is a separate plaque, which reads: 'County Borough of West Ham, Grove Gardens. Damaged during the Second World War, these gardens were restored to commemorate the Festival of Britain 1951. Mayor 1951–52 Councillor W.W. Paton JP.' The gardens have since been replaced by a hotel.

A memorial outside the library commemorates the poet Gerard Manley Hopkins (1844–1889) who was born and lived at No. 87 The Grove until 1852. He was the eldest of nine children. He died in 1889 and his house was destroyed during the Blitz.

Blue Plaques

Born in Birmingham, **Will Thorne** (1857–1946) moved to London in 1882 and worked as a stoker at Beckton Gas Works. He led the workers in a fight against increasing mechanisation and the introduction of an eighteen-hour shift. He founded the Gasworkers and General Labourers Union at a meeting in Canning Town in 1889, which recruited over 3,000 members within two weeks. The union won their fight for an eight-hour day. Thorne became secretary of the union. He later became a West Ham councillor and mayor, and in 1906 became Labour MP for West Ham South, a post he held until 1945. He was president of the TUC in 1912.

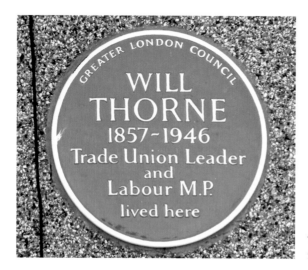

The blue plaque at Will Thorne's former home in Lawrence Road, E13.

Charlie Paynter (1879–1970) was manager of West Ham United FC from 1932 to 1950. This blue plaque is mounted at his former home in Ladysmith Avenue, E6.

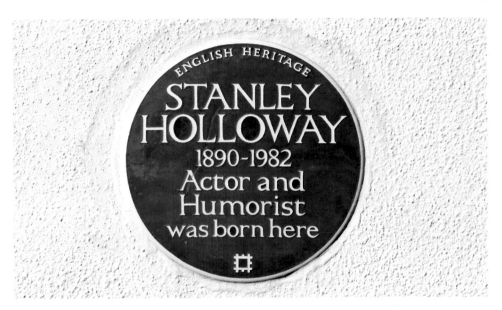

Stanley Holloway (1890–1982), actor and humorist, was born in Manor Park at No. 25 Albany Road, E12. He was the star of many of the famous Ealing comedies of the 1950s such as *Passport to Pimlico* and *The Titfield Thunderbolt*. The English Heritage blue plaque was installed in 2009.

Daisy Parsons (1890–1957) was born as Marguerite Lena Millo in Tower Hamlets. Her family moved to Canning Town before 'Daisy', as she was known, turned one. After leaving school aged twelve, her work experiences encouraged her to join the East London Suffrage Movement and to follow a political career. In 1922 she was elected a Labour councillor for Beckton. She would go on to become the first female mayor of West Ham in 1936. She was awarded the MBE in 1951 for public service. A blue plaque was placed on West Ham Town Hall by Newham Council in 2019.

Jack Leslie (1901–88), a Black footballer, was born in Canning Town and played for Barking Town and later Plymouth Argyle. In 1925 he was picked to play for England, but his name was dropped from the team sheet when officials discovered his Black heritage and he never received another call-up. After retiring from playing, he worked as a boot-boy at West Ham United for over fifteen years. A blue plaque was erected to his memory in 2021 at Gerald Road, Canning Town, and a new block of flats was named Jack Leslie Point in 2022.

A heritage blue plaque was erected in May 2021 at the site of the former **Upper Cut Club**, Woodgrange Road, Forest Gate to commemorate where Jimi Hendrix wrote the lyrics to 'Purple Haze' before his performance there on Boxing Day 1966. The Upper Cut Club opened in 1966 with The Who topping the bill. The building had originally been built in 1902 as a public hall, later becoming the Grand Theatre in 1907 and later a cinema. The Upper Cut Club only lasted until December 1967 after which the building remained empty until demolished *c.* 2005 and replaced by a ventilation shaft for the Channel Tunnel rail link, which passes below.

The plaque to Jimi Hendrix (1942–70) in Forest Gate.

Others

George Edwards (1694–1773) was known as the 'father of modern ornithology'. He wrote a four-volume treatise, *The History of Birds*, listing every then known species. He lived in Balaam Street, Plaistow.

Luke Howard (1772–1864), pharmacist and amateur meteorologist, lived at the Lock House, Three Mills. He proposed a naming system for clouds, which is still in use.

Edmund Burke (1792–97), statesman and writer, lived in Brunstock Cottage, Balaam Street, Plaistow, from 1759 to 1761.

Lord Lister (1827–1912), founder of antiseptic surgery, was born in Upton House, Upton Lane. In 1908 he was given the Honorary Freedom of the Borough of West Ham. Upton House was demolished in 1968.

Nina Layard (1853–1935), a botanist, antiquary, archaeologist, poet and prehistorian who made many important discoveries. She was born in Stratford and is commemorated by a street name there (see p. 9).

James Keir Hardie (1856–1915), the Scottish-born founder of the Labour Party, was first elected to Parliament as an Independent MP for West Ham South in 1892. He caused outrage by turning up at Parliament in a cloth cap and workman's suit. He was defeated in 1895, but later became the first Labour MP, representing Merthyr Tydfil, and the first chairman of the Parliamentary Labour Party.

Dame Vera Lynn (1917–2020), originally Vera Margaret Walsh, the 'Forces Sweetheart', was born in a house on Thackery Road, East Ham, E6. From 1921 to 1938 she lived in nearby Ladysmith Avenue, E6. Both these roads now have descriptive details on their street names. In addition, as previously mentioned, one of the latest Woolwich ferries is named after her.

Wag Bennett (1930–2008) was born in Canning Town and developed an interest in bodybuilding. He opened a gym at No. 335 Romford Road, Forest Gate, later acquiring the Emmanuel church hall next door as his base. He married Diane, who came from a gym-owning, bodybuilding family and who managed a troop of bodybuilders called Dianne Bennett's Glamour Girls. In 1966 the pair took on Arnold Schwarzenegger, a nineteen-year-old Austrian former army conscript who had taken up bodybuilding and come second in the Mr Universe competition. The Bennetts brought him to Forest Gate and helped him develop his career. Arnold won the Mr Universe competition in 1967. Arnold later moved to America and achieved great success in acting and subsequently politics. Luke Bennett, one of Wag Bennett's sons became an osteopath and runs the Liberty Clinic at No. 394 Romford Road, not far from his father's former gym.

DID YOU KNOW?
Other famous people born in Newham include the actors Reg Varney, Windsor Davies and Marty Feldman, actress Honor Blackman, actor/director Bryan Forbes, singer/actor David Essex, singer/songwriter Linda Lewis and scriptwriter Johnny Speight. More recently the actor Idris Elba, although born in Hackney, grew up in Newham. Also, the boxer Lennox Lewis was born in Stratford.

9. Parks, Green Spaces, Sport and Recreation, and Cemeteries

Central Park
Central Park, East Ham, was opened on the former site of Rancliffe House in 1898. The cost was £17,000.

Lyle Park
This was opened in 1924 and financed by the Lyle family whose sugar refinery was nearby.

Royal Victoria Park
Located by the river at North Woolwich, this opened in 1851 as the Royal Pavilion Gardens. This was the last of the many Victorian Pleasure Gardens to be created and had circus acts, music and dancing. Visitors would arrive by boat to North Woolwich Pier. However, it was in decline by the early 1880s. It was then taken into public ownership, redesigned and reopened under the present name in 1890.

Central Park Burges drinking fountain. This was unveiled at the opening in 1898 and designed with children in mind. The inscription reads: 'Dedicated to the children of East Ham by Colonel Burges, a Vice-Chairman of the Metropolitan Gardens Association, 5 July 1898.' His name is also commemorated by Burges Road, East Ham.

Central Park urns. There are four of these stone urns dating from *c.* 1929. They formerly decorated the clock tower of the London Co-operative store in East Ham, which stood on the opposite corner to the Town Hall and was demolished in 1989.

Stratford Park

Originally opened over a hundred years ago as the West Ham Lane Recreation Ground, taking its current name in 1998. It is located on the site of a former grand house named 'Senables' or 'Sanables', which stood until the eighteenth century. Many original features remain including the entrances, cast-iron railings and ornamental fountain.

West Ham Park

This park originated in the sixteenth century as the grounds of Grove House, later known as Rookes Hall and later still as Ham House. In the eighteenth century the eminent surgeon Dr John Fothergill turned the site into one of the finest botanical gardens in Europe. Ham House was demolished in 1872. At that time it was owned by the Gurney family, who sold the land in 1874 for use as a park. The park is managed not by Newham but by the Corporation of the City of London. It was formerly opened by the Lord Mayor of London on 20 July 1874. The title deeds declared the park 'open public grounds and gardens for adults, children and youth'. At 77 acres, this is the largest park in Newham and has its own nursery supplying plants for use in the park and other public spaces. This has been listed as a Grade II site on the English Heritage Register of Parks and Gardens of Specific Historic Interest in England.

Thames Barrier Park

Thames Barrier Park is a 7-hectare park in Silvertown located by the north bank of the Thames next to the Thames Barrier. This opened in November 2000 and was London's largest new riverside park for over fifty years. The site previously housed petrochemical and acid works and the contaminated soil was covered with a six foot layer of crushed concrete to protect the new soil laid on top. The park is managed by the Greater London Authority and has won design awards.

This cairn of stones in West Ham Park marks the site of the former Ham House.

A feature of Thames Barrier Park is the 'Green Dock', a 130-foot-long sunken garden that is intended as a reminder of the area's dockland heritage, having the appearance of being a former dry dock. Beyond this the Thames Barrier can be seen.

Queen Elizabeth Olympic Park

The latest addition to Newham's wealth of parks and open spaces, this was created by the London Legacy Development Corporation from part of the Olympic Park site. It is the largest new London park in over 100 years and spans parts of Newham, Tower Hamlets, Hackney and Waltham Forest. Within its boundaries are the London Stadium (formerly Olympic Stadium and now home to West Ham United), the London Aquatics Centre, Copper Box Arena, and Lee Valley VeloPark. The first stage opened in July 2013 when the site was renamed to commemorate the diamond jubilee of Elizabeth II. Most of the remainder reopened in April 2014.

The Greenway

Running diagonally across Newham from Stratford to Beckton is the Greenway, a long, narrow path popular with cyclists and joggers. This was built as part of the London sewer system designed by Sir Joseph Bazalgette in the 1860s. It covers the Northern Outfall Sewer, a gravity sewer running from Wick Lane, Hackney to the Beckton Sewage Works. The Greenway was upgraded in the run-up to the London Olympics for which it was designated an official walking route.

A view along the Greenway at West Ham with the original Abbey Mills Pumping Station, built to raise the sewage nearly 40 feet from the two low-level sewers, which join here to the Northern Outfall Sewer. Since a new pumping station was completed in 1997, this now only serves as a standby to deal with storm flows.

Wanstead Flats

Wanstead Flats is a southern part of Epping Forest and until the 1850s was known as the Lower Forest. Epping Forest had been a royal hunting ground until Stuart times, although local residents had the right to take wood and graze cattle. With the coming of the railways in the 1850s it was increasingly used as a place of recreation on Sundays and holidays by people from East London. However, by the 1860s it was under threat as individual landowners were making illegal enclosures and depriving the locals of their rights. By 1870 the unenclosed forest land had shrunk to only some 3,500 acres. In July 1871 thousands gathered in a protest demonstration against this – a campaign that the renowned ecologist Oliver Rackham would dub 'the origin of the modern British environmental movement'. This led to the involvement of the City of London Corporation who had purchased forest land for the construction of the City of London Cemetery. In 1874 enclosures made in the previous twenty years were declared illegal. Then, under the Epping Forest Act, 1878, the forest ceased to be a royal forest and was purchased by the City of London Corporation who were appointed the Forest's Conservators. This was the first piece of legislation authorising the public's right to use an open space in Britain for leisure.

The Forest now extends to some 6,000 acres in total. Much of Wanstead Flats has been largely treeless since the twelfth century when the abbots of Stratford grazed their flocks of sheep there. There have been football pitches provided since 1890. Much of the area is within the boundaries of the London Borough of Redbridge, with other parts coming within Newham and Waltham Forest.

A view of part of Wanstead Flats, just north of Manor Park station.

West Ham United FC, Boleyn Ground, Priory Road

Priory Road, Upton Park, was the site of the Boleyn Ground, the former home of West Ham United. The name arises because there was once an Upton Park House, which was also known as Boleyn Castle because it was supposedly owned, or had been stayed in, by Anne Boleyn. The grounds were rented to the Thames Ironworks football club, which in 1900 merged with two other amateur teams, St Luke's and the Old Castle Swifts, to became

New housing under construction in 2021 at Priory Road on the site of the former Boleyn Ground.

West Ham United. Arnold Hills, the owner of Thames Ironworks donated the money for the clubs to merge and turn professional. West Ham United played Bolton Wanderers in the first FA. Cup Final to be held at Wembley Stadium in 1923, losing 2-0. West Ham would achieve FA Cup success three times in 1964, 1975 and 1980, but perhaps their greatest moment was when three of their players – the captain Bobby Moore, Geoff Hurst and Martin Peters – were in the England squad that won the World Cup at Wembley in 1966. The club moved out of the Boleyn Ground in 2016 to become tenants of the former Olympic stadium at Stratford, now renamed the London Stadium, and the old football ground was sold off for housing.

This mural on the corner of Priory Road commemorates the former football ground.

The statue to the World Cup winners at Upton Park, opposite the Boleyn public house, erected in 2003. Former West Ham players Bobby Moore and Trevor Brooking have also been given street names in Newham – Moore Walk and Brooking Road.

The FA Cup

In October 1863 the representatives of twelve London and suburban football clubs met to form an association and establish a definite code of rules for the game. Eleven of the teams signed up and this was the beginning of the Football Association (FA). On 28 July 1871 the FA Secretary Charlie Alcock proposed having a Challenge Cup that all the Association members could compete for. This would be called the Football Association Challenge Cup or FA Cup for short. All fifty member clubs by then were invited but only fifteen replied and, following withdrawals, only twelve teams competed in the inaugural year.

The first ever FA Cup match to be played took place on 11 November 1871 in West Ham Park and was between Upton Park and Clapham Rovers (who won 3-0), watched by over 1,000 spectators. The final was played at Kennington Oval on 16 March 1872 between Wanderers and Royal Engineers in front of 2,000 spectators, Wanderers winning 1-0.

West Ham Stadium

This opened in 1928 and principally offered motor-cycle speedway racing and later greyhound racing, although football, baseball and athletics meetings were also held. The Stadium building could hold 40,000 spectators. The site closed in 1972. Initially the entrance gates in Nottingham Avenue were retained but were subsequently demolished. However, streets built on the site of the stadium were named after former speedway riders – Arthur Atkinson, Tommy Croombs, Johnnie Hoskins, Bluey Wilkinson and Jack Young.

The entrance to the former West Ham Stadium. (Photo courtesy of Newham Archives, Newham Heritage Service)

DID YOU KNOW?
At the 1936 Olympic Games, five members of the British water polo team came from Plaistow Swimming Club.

Cemeteries

Newham has seven cemeteries including two Jewish cemeteries. The oldest and largest is the City of London Cemetery and Crematorium. In 1849, with a growing London population the Commissioners of the City of London directed a cemetery to be built rather than burial within the parishes of London. The former farmland of the Manor of Aldersbook was purchased from the 2nd Duke of Wellington. The cemetery was opened in 1856 by the City of London Burial Board. The buildings and overall design were by William Haywood, architect to the City's Commissioners for Sewers. The landscaping was undertaken by Robert Davidson. The cemetery occupies 200 acres and it is estimated to have had nearly a million burials including reinterments from closed churches and those destroyed in the Blitz. A crematorium was added in 1904 and new crematorium was built in 1971. West Ham Cemetery followed in 1857, East London Cemetery in 1872 and Manor Park Cemetery in 1876.

The entrance gateway to the City of London Cemetery, the grounds of which are Grade I listed.

10. The Odd

Please Close the Gate

Forest View Road, Manor Park, fronts onto Wanstead Flats. There is housing on one side of the road only, a mixture of terraced housing and council flats. Until an outbreak of BSE in 1996 cattle were allowed to be grazed on the Flats. On the council blocks there are these now faded signs requesting residents to close the garden gates to prevent cattle from straying within. I cannot imagine there can many other places in Greater London where council flats have displayed similar notices.

Lost in Translation

This former furniture shop in Barking Road, East Ham, displayed some remarkable spelling mistakes and errors on its sign. The shop has since become an Asian-owned grocers and the sign has been replaced.

The sign on Forest View Road.

'Wardrobs' and 'chester drawers' available! Photographed in August 2020.

Abbey Road

There is an Abbey Road station on the Docklands Light Railway. There is also an Abbey Road crossing made famous in a Beatles album, but it is not this Abbey Road! Just in case any tourists turn up at the wrong site, Transport for London have installed this notice board with instructions of how to get to the real Abbey Road (near St John's Wood station) and with various references to Beatles lyrics.

Road to Nowhere

This bridge at Beckton, near Gallions Reach station, crosses the Docklands Light Railway and then just ends without the road continuing. Traffic can turn off on to a road to the left of the railway but cannot continue straight ahead. The view taken from the DLR shows how the bridge ends after crossing the approach roads to the DLR Beckton depot. This was originally built as an access to the projected Thames Gateway Bridge that was proposed by Transport for London in the early 2000s and supported by the then London Mayor, Ken Livingstone. The bridge would have crossed the Thames from Beckton to Thamesmead and would have had four lanes for general traffic, two lanes for public transport, a cycle lane, pedestrian walkway and facilities for a Docklands Light Railway crossing. There was a public enquiry into the proposals in 2005–06 with much opposition from environmental groups including Friends of the Earth. In July 2007 the planning inspector recommended that the bridge should not go ahead. The Secretary of State for Communities and Local Government requested that the public inquiry be reopened, but when the next London Mayor, Boris Johnson, came to office in 2008 the bridge was officially cancelled.

Abbey Road station, Docklands Light Railway.

The bridge at Beckton that abruptly ends.

Tea Up

A remarkable survival at East Ham station! The station was built by the London, Tilbury & Southend Railway and services transferred to the District Railway (now London Underground's District Line) in 1908. On the westbound platform is a building that was presumably at one time a refreshment room. Painted on the stonework at the top in three places is this 'Tea 2d a cup' lettering. There are also a number of surviving LT&SR bench seats and all the roof supports have this LTSR monogram scrollwork (seen here in reverse). Just outside the station there is also a water tower left over from when steam trains were still used on maintenance trains until 1971.

Drink Up

By Forest Gate station is this clock, water fountain and horse trough. This was installed in Victorian times by the Metropolitan Water Fountain and Horse Trough Association. This was originally established to provide free drinking water for Londoners and proved so successful that they also provided horse troughs for the horses that were then the prime motive power for transport. The association was founded by the Stratford banker and philanthropist Samuel Gurney. Like many of the Victorian philanthropists he was a supporter of the Temperance movement that campaigned against alcohol as a cause of social disorder and poverty. The location has been moved several times over the years and a gas lamp originally mounted above the clock has long gone.

Surviving painted stonework at East Ham station.

A clock, water fountain and horse trough all rolled into one!

Euston Arch

In 1962 Euston station in London was due to be rebuilt as part of the upgrade and electrification of the West Coast Main Line to Liverpool and Manchester. In a controversial move, the vast Doric arch built at the entrance in 1837 was demolished rather than being dismantled and relocated elsewhere. The ornamental iron gates were saved and are now at the National Railway Museum, York. In 1994 the historian Dan Cruickshank discovered that at least 60 per cent of the stones from the arch had been buried in the Prescott Channel, a back river of the River Lea at Stratford to fill a chasm in the bed of the channel. Many of the stones were removed in 2009 during upgrade work to make the Prescott Channel navigable for construction traffic to the Olympic Park. Dan Cruickshank launched the Euston Arch Trust, an organisation dedicated to the rebuilding of the arch. Although this has not happened to date, the reconstruction of the Euston area in connection with the building of HS2 has opened a possibility that this might happen in the future thus undoing what was seen by many as a monumental act of architectural vandalism.

DID YOU KNOW?
On 8–9 October 1988 the French musician Jean-Michel Jarre held a concert with fireworks and light show (Destination Docklands) in the former Royal Victoria Dock, attended by some 200,000 people. The light show used Second World War searchlights and lasers, lighting up the area like the incendiary bombs of wartime, and the electronic music could be heard from as far away as Manor Park.

Bibliography and Further Reading

Bloch, Howard, *Newham Dockland* (Stroud: Tempus, 1995)

Foley, Michael, *London's East End* (Stroud: Amberley, 2017)

Gorman, Mark & Peter Williams, *Forest Gate: A Short Illustrated History* (Forest Gate: Emporium 8, 2022)

Lund, Kenneth (comp), *Buildings in Newham* (London: London Borough of Newham, 1973)

Pewsey, Stephen, *Britain in Old Photographs: Stratford, West Ham & the Royal Docks* (Stroud: Sutton, 1996)

Sanders, Dorcas & Nick Harris, *Forest Gate* (Stroud: History Press, 2012)

The Newham Story: A Short History of Newham (London: London Borough of Newham, 2016)

The Islanders: The Industrial and Community Heritage of Silvertown and North Woolwich (Thames Festival Trust, 2021)

Websites

exploringeastlondon.co.uk – Exploring East London is an excellent website with maps created by the late Lawrence Rigal, who died in 2010. Although no longer being updated, the website remains available and is an ideal source for anyone wanting to explore the area, although some of the featured locations such as the North Woolwich Old Station Museum have since closed or been lost to redevelopment.

e7-nowandthen.org – a site devoted to the Forest Gate area.

hidden-london.com

londonremembers.com – devoted to charting all of London's memorials.

newhamheritagemonth.com

newhamphotos.com

newhamvoices.co.uk

Organisations

Eastside Community Heritage, hidden-histories.org

Docklands History Group, docklandshistorygroup.org.uk

Further Reading

Amies, Mark, *London's Industrial past* (Stroud: Amberley, 2020)

Barrett, Duncan and Nuala Calvi, *The Sugar Girls: Tales of Hardship, Love and Happiness in Tate & Lyle's East End* (London: Harper Collins, 2012)

Batten, Malcolm, *East London Railways: From Docklands to Crossrail* (Stroud: Amberley, 2020)

Batten, Malcolm, *London's Transport and the Olympics: Preparation, Delivery and Legacy* (Stroud: Amberley, 2022)

Gorman, Mark, *Saving the People's Forest: Open Spaces, Enclosure and Popular Protest in Mid-Victorian London* (University of Hertfordshire Press, 2021)

Hill, Graham & Howard Bloch, *The Silvertown Explosion London 1917* (Stroud: Tempus, 2004)

Joyce, J., *London Transport Bus Garages Since 1948* (Shepperton: Ian Allan, 1988)

McGrath, Melanie, *Silvertown: An East End Family Memoir* (London: Fourth Estate, 2002)

Marshall, Geoff, *London's Industrial Heritage* (Stroud: History Press, 2013)

Pedroche, Ben, *London's Lost Power Stations And Gasworks* (Stroud: History Press, 2013)

Ramsey, Winston G., *The East End Then and Now* (London: After the Battle, 1997)

'Unruly and Predatory Cattle': The Cows of Wanstead Flats (London: Leyton & Leytonstone Historical Society, 2022)

Acknowledgements

Thanks to Jess Conway, archivist at Stratford Library, for the use of photographs from the Newham Library Archives collection.